HIP-HOP

Hip-Hop

Kanye West

Rae Simons

Mason Crest Publishers

Kanye West

FRONTIS Kanye West is a good example of how hip-hop reaches beyond music. The megastar is shown here attending a 2004 benefit for arts education.

PRODUCED BY 21ST CENTURY PUBLISHING AND COMMUNICATIONS, INC.

EDITORIAL BY HARDING HOUSE PUBLISHING SERVICES, INC.

MASON CREST PUBLISHERS INC.
370 Reed Road
Broomall, Pennsylvania 19008
(866)MCP-BOOK (toll free)
www.masoncrest.com

Printed in Malaysia.

9 8 7 6 5 4 3 2

Library of Congress Cataloging-in-Publication Data

Simons, Rae.
    Kanye West / by Rae Simons.
        p. cm. — (Hip-hop)
    Includes bibliographical references (p.   ) and index.
ISBN 1-4222-0132-5 (alk. paper)
    1. West, Kanye—Juvenile literature. 2. Rap musicians—United States—
Biography—Juvenile literature. I. Title. II. Series.
ML3930.W42S56 2007
782.421649092—dc22   2006006588

Publisher's notes:
- All quotations in this book come from original sources, and contain the spelling and grammatical inconsistencies of the original text.

- The Web sites mentioned in this book were active at the time of publication. The publisher is not responsible for Web sites that have changed their addresses or discontinued operation since the date of publication. The publisher will review and update the Web site addresses each time the book is reprinted.

Contents

Hip-Hop Timeline

1974 Hip-hop pioneer Afrika Bambaataa organizes the Universal Zulu Nation.

1988 *Yo! MTV Raps* premieres on MTV.

1970s Hip-hop as a cultural movement begins in the Bronx, New York City.

1985 *Krush Groove*, a hip-hop film about Def Jam Recordings, is released featuring Run-D.M.C., Kurtis Blow, LL Cool J, and the Beastie Boys.

1970s DJ Kool Herc pioneers the use of breaks, isolations, and repeats using two turntables.

1979 The Sugarhill Gang's song "Rapper's Delight" is the first hip-hop single to go gold.

1986 Run-D.M.C. are the first rappers to appear on the cover of *Rolling Stone* magazine.

1970   1980   1988

1976 Grandmaster Flash & the Furious Five pioneer hip-hop MCing and freestyle battles.

1986 Beastie Boys' album *Licensed to Ill* is released and becomes the best-selling rap album of the 1980s.

1970s Break dancing emerges at parties and in public places in New York City.

1982 Afrika Bambaataa embarks on the first European hip-hop tour.

1988 Hip-hop music annual record sales reaches $100 million.

1970s Graffiti artist Vic pioneers tagging on subway trains in New York City.

1984 *Graffiti Rock*, the first hip-hop television program, premieres.

1993 Rapper Snoop Dogg's album *Doggystyle* is the first debut album to hit the music charts at number one.

2006 Queen Latifah becomes the first hip-hop artist to receive a star on the Hollywood Walk of Fame.

1989 DJ Jazzy Jeff & The Fresh Prince become the first hip-hop artists to win a Grammy Award.

2003 Rapper Eminem becomes the first hip-hop artist to win an Academy Award.

2005 Hip-hop artist Kanye West appears on the cover of *Time* magazine.

1989 Rap is added as a new category to the *Billboard* charts.

1997 East Coast rapper Notorious B.I.G. (aka Biggie Smalls) is murdered.

2004 First National Hip-Hop Political Convention is held in Newark, New Jersey.

1989   2000   2006

1990s Hip-hop emerges in Europe.

1996 West Coast rapper Tupac Shakur is shot and killed.

2005 Rapper Will Smith opens the Philadelphia Live 8 concert as part of 10 simultaneous concerts held worldwide to bring attention to the extreme poverty in Africa.

1989 First gangsta rap album, *Straight Outta Compton*, is released by N.W.A.

2001 The hip-hop political action group, Hip-Hop Summit Action Network, is founded by Russell Simmons.

2006 The Smithsonian Institute National Museum of American History announces the creation of a new hip-hop exhibition scheduled to open in three to five years.

1992 Dr. Dre's album *The Chronic* is released; it redefines West Coast rap.

The 47th Annual Grammy Awards in 2005 was a big event for Kanye West. Nominated for ten awards, Kanye won three Grammys. Both his talents as a singer and as a producer were honored—but according to Kanye, he should have won all ten awards.

1

And the Winner Is . . .

It was a night of music and all-star performances—and Kanye West was at the center of it all. On February 13, 2005, after being nominated for a total of ten Grammys, Kanye walked away with three. With Mavis Staples, John Legend, and the Blind Boys of Alabama, Kanye celebrated **rap** music's deepest roots in a moving rendition that showed the progression from Gospel to hip-hop.

If nothing else, Kanye West's success is a sure-fire sign that hip-hop has come a long way since its early beginnings in the streets of the South Bronx in New York City. In the 1970s, hip-hop was a **subculture** that belonged only to inner-city young people. Thirty-five years later, hip-hop's rhythm had gone mainstream. Kanye West's music proved that hip-hop could be popular—and still be true to its roots by rapping the truth in a voice too loud for anyone to ignore.

Kanye West would be hard to ignore—he has earned himself a sizeable reputation for both his talent and his outrageous comments—but his

Grammys made sure the world would not overlook him. The Grammy Awards are presented each year by the National Academy of Recording Arts and Sciences (NARAS), and most performers consider a Grammy to be the most coveted of the many contemporary music awards. Despite the honor the awards carry and the ratings success of the televised awards show, some industry insiders say the Grammys are merely a reflection of mainstream commercial success. But for a hip-hop artist like Kanye West, commercial success is all right—so long as he knows he's using that success to say something important to the world.

Kanye didn't seem surprised by the trophies he collected on that February night in 2005. "Everybody wanted to know what would I do if I didn't win. I guess we'll never know," he said, holding high a trophy. Later, he went so far as to say, "I got ten Grammy nominations, and won three—even if I should have won all ten." (Kanye has never been known for his modesty!)

Kanye West was the most nominated artist of 2005. His Grammy nominations were:

- Album of the Year for *The College Dropout*
- Album of the Year for his contributions to *The Diary of Alicia Keys*
- Song of the Year, for writing "Jesus Walks" (from his *Dropout* album), along with co-writer Rhymefest
- Best New Artist
- Best Rap Album for *The College Dropout*
- Best Rap Song, for writing "Jesus Walks" with co-writer Rhymefest
- Best **R&B** Song for co-writing Alicia Keys' "You Don't Know My Name," from *The Diary of Alicia Keys*
- Best Rap Solo Performance for "Through the Wire," from *Dropout*
- Best Rap/Sung Collaboration for "Slow Jamz" (also featuring Twista and Jamie Foxx), from *Dropout*
- Best Rap/Sung Collaboration for "All Falls Down" (featuring Syleena Johnson), from *Dropout*

In the end, Kanye walked away with Best Rap Album for *Dropout*, Best Rap Song, along with his long-time friend and fellow rapper Rhymefest, for the single "Jesus Walks," and Best R&B Song for producing Alicia Keys' "You Don't Know My Name."

When Kanye accepted his awards, he said:

"Y'all might as well get the music ready 'cause this is gonna take a while. When I had my accident, I found out at that moment, nothing in life is promised except death. If you have the opportunity to play this game called life, you have to appreciate every moment. A lot of people don't appreciate their moment until it's passed. . . . Right now, it's my time, and my moment, thanks to the fans, thanks to the accident, thanks to God, thanks to Roc-A-Fella [Records], Jay-Z, Dame Dash, G, my mother, Rhymefest, everyone that's helped me. And I plan to celebrate, and scream and pop champagne every chance I get, 'cause I'm at the Grammys, baby!"

Kanye was the most-nominated artist of the 47th Annual Grammy Awards. Kanye and other stars, including Mark McGrath, Earth Wind and Fire, Black Eyed Peas, Kevin Spacey, and Joss Stone, attended the nomination announcement in 2004.

In 2005, Kanye won an MTV Music Video Award for Best Male Video. His winning video was "Jesus Walks." One video for the song was not enough, at least in Kanye's mind—so he made three.

Kanye had come through hard times—but he'd never doubted that in the end he would triumph.

All in all, the year 2005 was a good one for Kanye West. The Grammys weren't the only recognition of his success. Later the same month, his hometown of Chicago declared February 27, 2005, to be Kanye West Day. So maybe Kanye can be excused for feeling just a little proud of himself.

Kanye (right) and actor Jamie Foxx (left) brought the house down and the audience to their feet with their performance of "Gold Digger" at the 48th Annual Grammy Awards on February 8, 2006. Kanye won the Grammy for Best Rap Solo Performance for "Gold Digger."

In a repeat of 2005, Kanye won three Grammy Awards in 2006. Here he is shown sharing the spotlight with his girlfriend (center) and mother (right). Kanye's mother, Donda West, has been a big influence on his success—and life.

When AllHipHop.com asked Kanye how he felt on Kanye West Day, he responded:

> **" I felt overwhelmed. My favorite artists from [Bumpy] Johnson to Common, Do or Die, GLC . . . performed a song that I produced for them, and then a song from my album, *College Dropout*. Rappers that I love were spitting my rap."**

2006 Grammy Awards

The year 2006 was pretty good to Kanye as well. He was nominated for eight Grammy awards—tied for the most with Mariah Carey and Kanye's own **protégé**, John Legend. Kanye's 2006 nominations included:

- Album of the Year for *Late Registration*
- Album of the Year for contributions to Mariah Carey's *The Emancipation of Mimi*
- Record of the Year for "Gold Digger" (featuring Jamie Foxx) from *Late Registration*
- Best Rap Album for *Late Registration*
- Best Rap Song for "Diamonds from Sierra Leone" from *Late Registration*
- Best Rap Solo Performance for "Gold Digger" from *Late Registration*
- Best Rap/Sung Collaboration for "They Say" (featuring John Legend and Common)
- Best R&B Song for co-writing Alicia Keys' "Unbreakable"

On February 8, 2006, Kanye won three awards: Best Rap Album for *Late Registration*, Best Rap Song for "Diamonds from Sierra Leone," and Best Rap Solo Performance for "Gold Digger."

Kanye's life had turned into a dream come true. But Kanye took his success in stride. After all, he fought hard to get where he is today—and giving up was never an option.

Kanye's mother often accompanies her son to award ceremonies, such as the 2005 Billboard Music Awards, shown here. Kanye credits her, a former English professor, with teaching him about the rhythms and emotion of language. Both his parents have supported Kanye's music career.

2

Where It All Began

Kanye Omari West had a sense of rhythm right from the start. He was born on June 8, 1977, in Atlanta, Georgia, but he grew up on the South Side of Chicago. His mother, Dr. Donda West, was an English professor and an **activist**. His father, Jay West, was a photojournalist with two master's degrees; he was also a member of the **Black Panthers**.

Kanye's parents gave him a sense of America's most important issues. His father taught him that **racism** was everywhere. His mother taught him that everyone can make a difference. She also gave him appreciation for the rhythms and emotion of language.

According to Donda West, her son was humming even before he could talk. "Even as a child in the stroller," she said, "he would use his two fingers [to tap out rhythms] and it seemed to me that the wheels were turning even when he was an infant."

THE BLACK PANTHER

INTERCOMMUNAL NEWS SERVICE

PUBLISHED WEEKLY BY THE BLACK PANTHER PARTY

copyright © 1977 by Huey P. Newton   VOL. XVI NO. 16   SATURDAY, FEBRUARY 26, 1977   25¢

Inside

- **Elaine Brown Honored By Fremont High School Students**
  RECEIVES PLAQUE AT AFRO-AMERICAN HISTORY ASSEMBLY   PAGE 3

- **Athletes Endorse Judge Wilson For Mayor Of Oakland**
  TOP PRESENT, FORMER PROFESSIONAL SPORTSMEN HOLD PRESS CONFERENCE   PAGE 7

- **FRELIMO Reorganizes As A Vanguard Political Party**
  SAMORA MACHEL CALLS FOR "IRON ORGANIZATION AND DISCIPLINE"   CENTERFOLD

- **Foreign Leaders Bribed With C.I.A. Payoffs**
  PROJECT "NO BEEF" EXPOSES PAYMENTS TO DOZENS OF HEADS OF STATE   PAGE 17

Oakland Community School Performance

"REMEMBERING OUR ROOTS" CELEBRATES BLACK HISTORY

Oakland Community School Director ERICKA HUGGINS (above) and scenes from the School's special Black history celebration held last Sunday.

(Oakland, Calif.) — In celebration of Black History Month, the talented children of the Oakland Community School (OCS) presented an original five-act play entitled *Remembering Our Roots* on Sunday, February 20, at the Oakland Community Learning Center.

Following a welcome from OCS Director Ericka Huggins, *Remembering Our Roots* got underway. The play was appropriately named as it traced the history of Black people in America from their abduction from Africa into slavery up to the present. As is always the case for OCS productions, the play was written by the children themselves.

The play was presented as an "Oakland Community School News Special," and news commentators were Jackie Logan, Walter Butler and Glen Thornton. Jackie began by explaining that the history of Black Americans started in Africa.

Next, the boys and girls of Levels 4-7, ages six through 11, presented an Azanian (South African) warrior chant and dance that is used as a warning in a test of skills. The children received several rounds of applause from the audience during their polished performance of the warrior dance, taught to them by the creative OCS Artist-in-Residence, Ms. Thoko-Mondlase Hall, whose home is Azania.

Following the warrior dance, the girls of Levels 4-7 performed another Azanian chant and dance. The young sisters' rhythmic, soulful movements across the stage reminded everyone present of the roots of Black

CONTINUED ON PAGE 6

Kanye's father, Ray, was a member of the Black Panthers. Active from the late 1960s to early 1970s, the Black Panthers was a controversial African American political group. Its goal was to end white domination and better the lives of African Americans.

Kanye had a lot going for him—but he also faced the challenges that any kid faces, particularly a black kid growing up in Chicago. When he was eight or nine, a group of older boys tried to make off with his bicycle; when Kanye refused to give up his wheels, the other boys pulled out knives and slashed his tires. But Kanye's spirit didn't break easily.

His father, Ray West, credits his father-in-law Buddy with imparting his proud spirit to Kanye. "Buddy is a true Muhammad Ali fan," Ray told *Rolling Stone.* Apparently, Kanye's grandfather likes to strut and boast, just like his hero, boxer Muhammad Ali. Ray says that Kanye's grandfather "will tell you in a minute that he's the best thing to ever come along."

An Entertainer from the Start

Back when Kanye was a child, his mother was a visiting professor at Nanjing University in China. Kanye went with her and used his smooth moves to earn himself ice cream money by putting on spur-of-the-moment martial arts displays in the streets. Passersby would throw him coins—and Kanye loved every minute of it. His mother, however, was not as pleased. Kanye told Britain's *NME* magazine: "My mother was like, 'How can you ask for money from these poor Chinese people?' I guess I was a hustler in fifth grade, entertaining people."

When Kanye and his mother returned to the United States, kids teased him and called him "China Boy"—but the entertainment bug had bitten Kanye. Now, though, he turned his attention away from martial arts to music. At twelve, he convinced his mother to give him $25 to record his first song, "Green Eggs and Ham." By the time he was fourteen, he was saving all his allowance money to get **samplers** for his computer. He also persuaded his mother to loan him the money he needed to buy an expensive keyboard, and he started hanging out at clubs, where he could surround himself with the sound of hip-hop (even though technically, he was too young to be in the clubs).

Goals for the Future

Kanye was determined that he was going to be the next hip-hop superstar. As an adult, he remembered, "I thought I was going to get signed back when I was thirteen years old, and come out with a record and take Kris Kross out." (Kris Kross was a 1990s kiddie rap group.)

Throughout Kanye's years at Eisenhower High School, he enjoyed basketball, lunch, and gym—and he endured the rest of the school day. Other kids teased him for his braces and his Chiclets-sized teeth; Kanye put up with that as well.

What really excited him at school was music, and he focused on all the musical opportunities his school offered. He also experimented with poetry, while outside of school, he immersed himself in the music of classic rappers like Run-DMC. "All I ever wanted to do was help people and make music," he said. His struggles and frustrations growing up would one day inspire the lyrics for his first album.

As an adult, Kanye's childhood stayed fresh in his mind. He would use the Chicago skyline as the backdrop for his concert stage, and his childhood hangouts often figured in his music videos. His loyalty to his school friends would mean that many of them ended up on his payroll. As much as his childhood in Chicago meant to him, though, when the time came for him to strike out on his own, Kanye had the self-confidence to make that difficult decision.

College Dropout

After high school, Kanye was accepted into the fine arts program at Chicago State University, where his mother was an English professor. Music was still the most important thing in his life, however, and new opportunities were coming his way. Being a student took up time and energy—and so did his music career. Kanye knew something had to give. He couldn't offer his best to either piece of his life when he felt as though he were being cut down the middle.

His mother had mixed feelings about him giving up on his college education. "We went back and forth," she said later, "and he was able to convince me that it was more important to follow his dreams." She gave her son her support and became his manager.

Kanye's father was also proud of his son, but he had problems with the way Kanye used bad language when he rapped. Ray West told *Rolling Stone*:

> **"I've stated to him very clearly that he needs to move beyond the negative language. . . . It's all right . . . on the corner, but when you start operating on a different level you can't talk like that. Fine, you're trying to get some street acceptance. [But] . . . get back to your roots.**

You know that's not where you came from. You know that's not how you were raised. **"**

Still, despite their reservations, Kanye's parents have clearly been a major element in his self-confidence. Their belief in him, ever since he was a child, inspired him to believe in himself as well.

Run-DMC was one of hip-hop's earliest and biggest success stories. Shown in this 2001 photo are (left to right) Darryl (DMC) McDaniel, Joseph (Run) Simmons, and Jason (Jam Master Jay) Mizell. Jam Master Jay was murdered in a shooting outside a recording studio in 2002.

After much soul-searching, Kanye decided to quit college to pursue his music career. This doesn't mean he thinks everyone should be a dropout, though. Kanye participates in many programs that encourage kids to stay in school and get an education.

Columbia Records

When Columbia Records dangled a deal in front of Kanye's nose, he was sure his career was on its way. Unfortunately, this time Kanye's brash confidence may have cost him the deal. He told Columbia Record's executive officer, Michael Mauldin, "I'm going to be bigger than Michael Jackson, I'm going to be bigger than Jermaine Dupri." What Kanye didn't know was this: Mr. Mauldin was Dupri's father. "We'll call you," Mr. Mauldin said.

But they didn't.

Kanye didn't give up his dream, though. His own music wasn't opening hip-hop's door to fame for him—so for the time being, he used his production skills.

Though it wasn't easy to get a break, Kanye finally got his first record contract. His music—a blend of hip-hop with a dose of ordinary life—brought forth a new media superstar, one like none that had been seen before.

3

Riding the Rainbow

Most everyone has dreams. We all imagine what it would be like if we could cross the magic rainbow that spans the distance between our hum-drum lives and the world of our dreams. Like Dorothy in *The Wizard of Oz*, we wish we could escape the dull routines of ordinary life—but most of us don't have the courage to try to walk the rainbow.

Kanye West, however, had a vision for his life: he believed that the stuff of everyday life could be transformed into something new and amazing—and that confidence was the rainbow that led him to fame. "Set your own goals in life," he said. "Don't let anyone dictate to you what you need to do."

A New Voice in Hip-Hop

Just because Kanye dropped out of college, didn't mean he thought that was the right thing for everyone, and he wasn't saying that education and deep thinking aren't important. Instead, he brought a whole new level of morality and meaning to hip-hop. **Gangsta rap** had been drawing a lot of attention with its obscenities and descriptions of crime and violence, but Kanye stood for something new. His songs looked at ordinary life and took it a step further. "Just think about whatever you've been through in the past week," he said, "and I have a song about that."

Rapper Ma$e said of Kanye:

> **"I appreciate people like Kanye, people that dare to be different. Hip-hop is supposed to be an avenue of expression, and people are supposed to be able to express what they feel, what they believe."**

By being true to what he believed, Kanye's music dared to be different. He created a new mix of hip-hop and ordinary life and laid the foundation for a fresh approach to rap music.

Kanye said:

> **"In music and society people tell you to pick a side. Are you mainstream or underground? Do you rhyme about nice cars, or about riding the train? Are you ignorant or do you know something about history? But I'm a person who can do all these different things. It's like everybody is taking the fork in the road. They don't see the rainbow in the middle. And I'm about to ride that. I'm the prism. And my music comes out in colors."**

The Door to Success

Like Oz's wizard, Kanye started off working his musical magic from behind the scenes, hidden by the production booth. Unlike the wizard, however, Kanye's magic was the real deal. When he was only twenty, he coproduced tracks for Harlem World and the Mad Rapper, but he caught his real break when his style caught the attention of Jay-Z's Roc-A-Fella Records. Kyambo "Hip-Hop" Joshua and G. Roberson at Roc-A-Fella were also blown away by Kanye's passionate production skills. He used **vintage** R&B samples and live instrumentation to give his work an emotion and sense of honesty that was unique to him alone.

One of Kanye's biggest breaks as a producer came when he caught the attention of hip-hop legend Jay-Z, shown here with Kanye in 2005. According to Kanye, working on Jay-Z's "Izzo (H.O.V.A.)" was a "turning point" in his life and career.

Kanye's career as a producer for Jay-Z's record company, Rock-A-Fella, was nothing short of a monumental success. Major hip-hop stars wanted him to produce their music. Eventually, Rock-A-Fella signed him to record his own music. Former clients, such as Twista (right), became fellow performers.

Kanye provided the beat to Jay-Z's smash hit "Izzo (H.O.V.A.)." "That was the turning point in my life," Kanye told Rap News Network.

❝ Jay made all the difference. I can't say that I wouldn't have done it without him, but he made it easier because he gave me the stamp, he gave me the streets. The Roc-A-Fella chain helped me get my name. ❞

On Jay-Z's now-classic album *The Blueprint*, Kanye drew from a variety of old music—the Jackson 5, the Doors, and the Temptations—

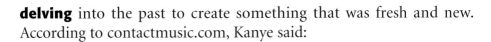

delving into the past to create something that was fresh and new. According to contactmusic.com, Kanye said:

> **"I feel like a lot of the soul that's in those old records that I sample is in me. So when I hear 'em and I put 'em to the new millennium it's just like God's doing that. I'm one with them records right there. It's a blessing."**

Kanye's work with Jay-Z soon made him the most in-demand hip-hop producer, and he went on to produce chart-topping hits for hip-hop's best and brightest artists, including Talib Kweli, Ludacris, Alicia Keys, Cam'ron, Scarface, Jamie Foxx, Twista . . . and the list goes on and on. The hip-hop world was paying attention to Kanye. "He's definitely put his foot in the game with his style of music," said Twista. "He's the beat man."

Kanye was eager for Roc-A-Fella to sign him as a recording artist in his own right, but initially, the record label was reluctant. Kanye with his pink polo shirts didn't seem to have the right image for hip-hop; he seemed too clean, not rough enough for real rapping. They didn't want to lose his productions skills, though, and finally they signed him as a performer.

It looked as though Kanye was shooting right to the top. In fact, in 2002 when he bumped into media mogul Oprah Winfrey while he was in New York City, he was so confident about his future that he told Oprah, "I'm going to be on your show one day." Oprah wasn't all that impressed; after all, people are always telling Oprah Winfrey about their claim to fame. But Kanye knew he was the real thing. Nothing was going to stand in his way.

Until a car accident turned his world upside down.

An almost-fatal car accident in 2002 was life changing for Kanye. It caused him to reflect on the "what might have been" and the "what could be" of his career—and more important, of his life.

4

Breakthrough

In October of 2002, while Kanye was driving back to his hotel in Los Angeles after a late-night recording session, he was involved in a car accident that was nearly fatal. "I have flashbacks of what happened every day," Kanye told the Roc-a-Fella Records Web site. "And any-time I hear about any accident, my heart sinks in and I thank God that I'm still here. I found out how short life is and how blessed you are to be here."

Through the Wire

The accident left Kanye with the bones in his face fractured in three places. Recovery was slow and painful—but Kanye was far from defeated. He turned to music to make sense out of the experience, and he used his creativity to rise above the pain. What's more, he wanted to do good with his music. "God spared my life not only to do music," he told AllHipHop.com, "but to use my powers to make things better for other people."

In the hip-hop world, producers aren't supposed to be the rappers on their own songs. But Kanye's never been one to pay much attention to "supposed-to-be." Stevie Wonder had produced his own music; so had other music greats like Prince, Tyrone Davis, and Bobby Womac. So why shouldn't Kanye? He went ahead and produced, wrote, and performed his own lyrics.

With his jaw wired shut, he wrote the story of his experience and recorded the single "Through the Wire." The song's chorus featured Kanye's trademark sound, a sped-up sample of a soul classic; in this case, Chaka Khan's "Through the Fire" provided an appropriate backdrop for Kanye's experience, as well as a play on words.

And then Kanye took a leap of faith. He financed and shot his own video of the song and delivered it to MTV and BET himself. Against the odds, the track became a breakout hit and marked his emergence as an important new hip-hop voice in his own right. Eventually, at long last, Kanye's premier album, *College Dropout*, was released in 2004.

Initially, the record was greeted with criticism. Its title sounded as though he was recommending that students walk away from educational opportunities. In a world where many blacks found it difficult to compete because of their lack of education, Kanye's title didn't seem to make a lot of sense.

Kanye responded to the criticism with a proud certainty that while education is vital, it can take many forms. He told AllHipHop.com:

"I feel that college is a choice, and anything you have to pay for is a choice. [But] high school is a necessity and these kids need every chance they can to survive because it is a hard world, just to say the least. . . . I was born to educate and fight for what I feel is right and just."

Confidence and Faith

Kanye was confident his album would be a success. He told the Associated Press:

"It's definitely a classic, if I stepped aside from myself and say that. . . . We'll see the results in the next six months, of whether it did change the game or whether it is its own entity."

Is Kanye West outrageous? Maybe. But, he always puts on a good show. Kanye is shown here performing his hit "Jesus Walks" at the 47th Annual Grammy Awards in 2005. "Jesus Walks" won the Grammy for Best Rap Song.

Statements like that earned Kanye a reputation for arrogance. Turns out, though, that he was right about his album. And he didn't just sit back and wait to see what happened. Instead, he *made* things happen.

His single "Slow Jamz," which he had recorded with Jamie Foxx and Twista on the *Dropout* album, became a number-one hit. "I'm trying to break radio, not make radio," Kanye told the press again and again—and the final hammer blow he used to smash into radio was his controversial single "Jesus Walks."

The song revealed that more than just self-confidence had helped Kanye reach his goals; he'd also relied on his faith. Kanye offered up his belief in God to hip-hop's rhythms, breaking the **stereotypes** that said rappers were all **materialistic** and violent. Then he went on to showcase the song in three different videos—and these were what rocketed Kanye to full-blown fame. The videos show Jesus walking along with a Ku Klux Klan (KKK) member, drug dealers, and various other "sinners," including Kanye himself.

One video shows Kanye as a rapping preacher in a church, with a choir singing in the background. During the sermon, an alcoholic, a thug, and a prostitute all "come forward" to meet Christ at the front altar of the church. "That was the first one he did," said Kanye's mother, Donda West, in an interview with *Relevant* magazine. "Kanye is so very passionate about this song, and he's also a **perfectionist**. He wanted to say something in these videos to reach people, and you can really relate to this video if you are from that tradition."

A second, more edgy, video shows KKK members burning a cross, doves flying into the air, and drug dealers running from the law. Mrs. West said, "It's healing . . . for all people who have been persecuted in a direct way, like racism. When you see Jesus even walking with a Klan member, who is so entrenched in hate, you can see that redemption is for everyone."

According to *Relevant* magazine, Kanye was the director of the third video, where a bushy-bearded Jesus hangs around the rapper for a regular day in his hometown of Chicago. This video is less flashy, more personal; it shows Jesus tapping on an empty refrigerator that becomes filled with food.

Fame and Fortune

The months that followed the release of "Jesus Walks" were a whirlwind of awards and live performances. *Dropout* was awarded the Grammy

AUGUST 29, 2005

Fall Preview Issue: Our Critics' Picks

IS THIS THE
FACE-OFF FOR '08?

TIME

HIP-HOP'S

CLASS ACT

Defying the rules of rap,
KANYE WEST
goes his own way.
Why he's the smartest
man in pop music
BY JOSH TYRANGIEL

www.time.com AOL Keyword: TIME

For Kanye, 2005 was a banner year. Not only was he super hot in the music scene, his story appeared in such mainstream publications as *Time* magazine. It seemed as though you couldn't pass a newsstand without seeing his face looking back at you.

for the Best Rap Album of 2005, and "Jesus Walks" got the Grammy for the Best Rap Song. The *New York Times, Time* magazine, *Rolling Stone, GQ, Spin, Blender, The Source,* and *XXL* all named *Dropout* Album of the Year. Kanye's fame was skyrocketing, and the money was rolling in—but he had also helped gain a new and more positive reputation for hip-hop.

It wasn't long before big business decided to cash in on the popularity of hip-hop—and of Kanye West. High-tech computer graphics and special effects—straight out of Hollywood movies and video games—joined Kanye in his commercial for Pepsi.

Kanye knew he was doing something different. He told Rap News Network:

> **"Every rapper was the king of . . . 'I can do this and not go to jail,' you know what I'm saying? Mine just came out from a totally different perspective. . . . I always want to do something different from what everybody else is doing, ever since I was little."**

Even hip-hop's greatest and most established musicians recognized Kanye's achievement. Usher chose Kanye for the coveted spot as his opening act on his tour. "I feel like Kanye, he thinks outside of the box," Usher said.

Kanye knew he had truly arrived when his face appeared on the cover of *Time* magazine. Before long, the advertising world was paying attention as well. After all, in a single year, according to American Bandstand, Kanye mentioned nineteen name brands in his music, including Lexus, Versace, Cartier, Mercedes, and Cadillac.

Like other rappers, Kanye mentioned these products not because he was paid to do so, but because they are a part of life—and hip-hop is a reflection of what's popular. Nevertheless, Kanye (and other hip-hop artists) were proving to the advertising world that rapping could be a useful sales tool. Big business, including McDonald's Corporation paid attention, and began considering musicians like Kanye to promote their businesses. Kanye had helped hip-hop gain the recognition of advertisers like McDonald's Douglas Freeland, who for the first time acknowledged that hip-hop is the "most dominant youth culture in the world."

Talk show hosts also recognized Kanye's new power. In 2005, Kanye's prediction to Oprah Winfrey came true, and he was asked to be a guest on her show. In fact, he made talk show history: he was the first person to have predicted to Oprah his own rise to fame. Later in 2005, Barbara Walters also interviewed Kanye on ABC's *Most Fascinating People of the Year*. Walters said of Kanye:

> **"His music doesn't glorify guns nor objectify girls. His songs are politically charged rhymes about say the horrors of the African diamond trade or the toll of drug abuse in America."**

Kanye responded: "I get away with it because I hide it behind really good beats—or hot things that make you laugh to keep from crying."

Arrogance and Creativity

With so much success coming his way, Kanye could have taken time off to simply gloat a little—but he didn't. Of course, he did do his share of boasting; Kanye's never been known for his soft-spoken modesty. In fact, just the opposite: he continues to earn quite a reputation for the size of his ego. Kanye, however, doesn't understand why that's a problem. "In America," he told *Rolling Stone*, "they want you to accomplish these great feats. . . . You want me to be great, but you don't ever want me to say I'm great?"

From Kanye's perspective, it would be dishonest for him not to admit his own achievements. "My thing is," he said on Rap News Network, "how can I possibly be overly confident? Look at my accomplishments!"

In a February 2006 interview, *Entertainment Weekly* asked Kanye if he was bothered by the conceited reputation he had earned for himself. Kanye explained where some of his pride comes from . . . and admits that he's struggling to learn humility.

> **❝There are times when I have leeway to spaz out because I'm a successful artist, but I really am trying my best not to be a jerk. I'm definitely a better person than I was two years ago. It's hard coming in—that struggle to get through the gate and everybody's dissing you, A&R people saying, 'You're never going to make it! No one's ever going to play this track!' People talk to you the way guards talk to prisoners. So for me to finally make it, I felt like I was fresh out of jail. And you know I got to go back to the people who used to bring me down. . . . I'm trying to take the power out of their words and give it back to me.❞**

Kanye also admits that a lot of his bragging and boasting is just an act to help him achieve his goals. He told Rap News Network:

> **❝A lot of times, arrogance is to combat insecurity. So in order for me to go out and do what I've done, facing**

Kanye had predicted he would win at the 2006 Grammys—and sure enough, he did (although he did not win Album of the Year as he had hoped). At a post-Grammy party, Kanye took the opportunity to gloat just a little on camera.

insecurity and facing people telling me I couldn't do it, I had to build a force field around myself. I had to be a borderline lunatic to think that I could do what I've done. It's crazy ... what I've accomplished is crazy.**"**

Kanye's creative craziness is still going strong. In 2005, he enlisted the help of composer/producer Jon Brion to create yet another album, *Late Registration*. This collection is a mix of new flavors and voices, and includes some old friends as well; Jay-Z, Jamie Foxx, Brandy, Paul Wall, Cam'ron, Adam Levine (of Maroon Five), and John Legend all have parts in the album. Kanye's not afraid to collaborate with the best and brightest stars in the hip-hop sky—but his sound remains uniquely his own.

Music's Positive Force

The album's themes tackle both personal and political issues. The single "Crack Music" looks at the effects of drugs on the black community. In

According to critics, Kanye's star appeal isn't the only thing that is supersized—so is his ego. However, Kanye always remembers his fans. Here, he is autographing copies of his 2005 release *Late Registration* for fans in a New York City record store.

"Heard 'Em Say," Adam Levine and Kanye stress the importance of honesty. "Gold Digger," which Kanye performs with Jamie Foxx, reminds listeners not to confuse love and money. Some of the tracks show Kanye's frustration, his sense of being an outsider in a white world, but most of the songs transform rage into something positive. Kanye uses the music to stand up loud and proud. It conveys the message that music and creativity can help heal the very real problems that challenge America.

He told Roc-A-Fella Records' Web site:

> **"It's hard when people are depending on you to have an album that's not just good, but inspired. I mean, my music isn't just music—it's medicine. I want my songs to touch people, to give them what they need. Every time I make an album, I'm trying to make a cure for cancer, musically. That stresses me out!"**

Clearly, Kanye takes his responsibilities seriously. Some people (the same people who criticize the size of Kanye's ego) might say Kanye takes himself *too* seriously. But Kanye is undeniably talented—and that talent gives him a platform, a place where he can stand up tall and do good in the world.

Music isn't the only way that Kanye is making his stand, however. He has also started a variety of businesses; he speaks his mind loud and clear on controversial political issues; and he's actively involved in charities, working hard to make the world a better place.

Kanye appreciates that musicians who came before him helped him reach his superstar status. Now firmly established in his career, Kanye is taking his turn as a mentor. Grammy-winner John Legend (left) is just one of the young musicians who has benefited from Kanye's experience.

5

Making a Mark

When Kanye West was growing up, he had plenty of goals: "To be gold or platinum, to have songs that are respected across the board, to have some sort of influence on the culture and to change the sound of music and inspire up-and-coming artists to go against the grain." By the time he was twenty-eight, he had achieved them all.

Businessman

Kanye's success doesn't mean he's relaxing, though. These days Kanye is using his outspoken confidence to promote more than just his own musical career.

For one thing, he's started his own fashion line, as well as his own music label, Getting Out Our Dreams (G.O.O.D.), which he's using to **mentor** new artists. The first musician he signed was the young up-and-coming hip-hopper John Legend. Kanye has acted as Legend's mentor, helping the young performer establish his career. "He has a reputation as having a big ego," Legend told TheAge.com, "but he's actually really easy to work with. When it comes to collaborating, he's actually always nothing but a gentleman." Apparently, John Legend has learned a lot from having Kanye as his role model. "I needed to have the resolve to combat others not believing in me," Legend said. "But you also have to have the humility to listen to other people and be able to take advice."

Charity

"God put me in a position to bring change," Kanye told AllHipHop.com. "I would be doing a disservice not to use this gift I have." So Kanye started his own foundation: the Kanye West Foundation, which works to keep minority students from dropping out of school. The foundation's first **initiative** was a program called Loop Dreams, designed to keep musical instruments in public schools. The program, which piloted in five schools in the fall of 2005, provides opportunities for at-risk students to learn how to write and produce music while improving their academic skills at the same time. Kanye hopes to expand Loop Dreams to schools nationwide by 2010. The Kanye West Foundation also hooked up with retail chain Musicland to launch a nationwide campaign to give a lucky student $150,000 toward the cost of a four-year college education.

In a February 2006 interview with *Entertainment Weekly*, Kanye said:

> **"My greatest talent, more so than being a rapper, is the ability to produce, to grab things that seem like they don't belong and put them together. I love building things, all the labor and refining and fine-tuning."**

Clearly, Kanye has the ability to get good things done. He has worked with Hip-Hop Summit Action Network (HSAN) to encourage young adults to vote and get more involved in politics. Kanye also performed with Live 8, a series of concerts that were given around the world on July 2, 2005, to raise awareness of Africa's extreme poverty. After Hurricane Katrina struck the Gulf Coast at the end of August 2005, Kanye visited the Reliant Center in Houston, Texas, to help cheer up children from New Orleans who had been uprooted from their homes. And aside from all these things Kanye has done, he constantly speaks out on behalf of justice, challenging people to take a new look at America's politics and beliefs.

Like other hip-hop artists, Kanye is doing his share to "give back." He is shown here performing at Live 8, a series of concerts held in 2005 that called for an end to the extreme poverty blanketing much of Africa.

Speaking from the Heart

Kanye's never been shy—and he's not afraid to speak his mind. In fact, he sees his outspoken honesty as a responsibility, especially when it comes to political issues. He told *Entertainment Weekly*:

❝When you stand up for any form of civil rights, you put yourself in the line of fire. But I feel like I'm here to change people's hearts and minds, to say something that's right for a change. And it goes all the way down the line, from telling people to stop being so **cliché**, to stop saying what you think your record label wants you to say, to stop giving drab acceptance speeches. Speaking from the heart is so much more than entertaining.❞

After the devastation of Hurricane Katrina, Kanye visited evacuees at the Reliant Center in Houston in September 2005. Kanye wanted to do what he could to comfort the families who had lost so much because of the hurricane.

After Hurricane Katrina ravaged America's Gulf Region, Kanye West's outspokenness stirred up a hornet's nest of controversy. As one of the narrators for an NBC special, "Concert for Hurricane Relief," Kanye startled viewers with his ad-lib comments. "I hate the way they portray us in the media," he said, referring to the media's portrayal of African Americans in New Orleans. "If you see a black family it says they are looting; if you see a white family it says they are looking for food. And you know, it's been five days [waiting for federal help] because most of the people are black."

Kanye was honest about his own feelings of anguish and helplessness.

"And even for me to complain about it, I would be a hypocrite because I've tried to turn away from the TV because it's too hard to watch. I've even been shopping before even giving a donation, so now I'm calling my business manager right now to see what is the biggest amount I can give."

But Kanye's final statement was what truly blew his viewers' minds: "George Bush doesn't care about black people," he stated bluntly.

These weren't comments that Kanye made lightly. His voice was shaky as he spoke, as though his own passion and bravery had terrified

Kanye went "off script" and criticized the government during a national telethon to benefit the victims of Hurricane Katrina. Here, he is shown covering his mouth at a post-telethon appearance. According to Kanye, he was not allowed to say anything this time.

him. But NBC was less than delighted by Kanye's impromptu comments. It issued a statement after the show, indicating:

"Kanye West departed from the scripted comments that were prepared for him, and his opinions in no way represent the view of the network. It would be most unfortunate if the efforts of the artists who participated tonight and the generosity of millions of Americans who are helping those in need are overshadowed by one person's opinion."

Many viewers, however, welcomed Kanye's willingness to speak his mind. "It was definitely a courageous move," Aaron McGruder, creator of the popular hip-hop comic *The Boondocks*, told *Rolling Stone*.

"He didn't know what the ramifications would be. He didn't know if it would end his career, and you could see all that on his face. You're not just dissing another rapper. You're dissing the president of the United States. That's real beef."

Not everyone, however, admired Kanye's courage. His statements outraged **conservatives** across the country. Many of Kanye's fellow rappers expressed their disapproval as well.

Rapper 50 Cent told ContactMusic.com that he disagreed with Kanye's statements. "I think people responded to it [the hurricane] the best way they can," 50 Cent said. "What Kanye West was saying, I don't know where that came from." Unlike Kanye, 50 Cent didn't blame the Bush administration for the destruction left in Hurricane Katrina's wake. Instead, 50 Cent said, "The New Orleans disaster was meant to happen. It was an act of God."

Hip-hop star Usher also made a public statement about Kanye's remarks:

"I wasn't mad at Kanye's statement—that's his opinion—but it's obviously not the opportunity or the time to poke fun or appoint blame. This is an opportunity where we all need to come together—musicians, actors, politicians—and help the Gulf region."

Though many criticized him for his comments regarding the government's Katrina relief efforts, fellow rapper Usher (left) supported Kanye's right to say what he did, giving him credit for opening a national dialogue about poverty and race in America.

Later, however, Usher modified what he had said with this statement:

"Contrary to false media reports, I support the personal opinions made by my friend Kanye West. If it wasn't for his comments, there would not be an open dialogue about the undeserved people in the gulf region."

Other stars, however, were even more up front about their support of Kanye. Kanye's old friend Jay-Z said:

"I'm backing Kanye 100 percent. This is America. You should be able to say what you want to say. We have freedom of speech. [The slow response to the disaster] is really numbing. You can't believe it's happening in America. You wonder, what's going on? Why were people so slow to react? I don't understand it."

Hip-hop megastar P. Diddy (shown here in the center, along with Kanye and Kelly Clarkson) also supported Kanye during the uproar caused by his telethon remarks. P. Diddy was certain the young artist had spoken from his heart.

Hip-hop superstar P. Diddy agreed:

"I think he spoke from his heart. He spoke what a lot of people feel. . . . It ain't adding up, man. It's not making sense. If the reporters can get there and you all can get there with microphones, somebody should be able to get there with food."

And actor Matt Damon chimed in with praise for Kanye:

"This guy with his moment on live television made a statement that hopefully now Bush will come out and address, because he doesn't have to address anything else. . . . The White House Press Corp, they should all have their credentials taken away. Not one of them's an honest journalist. Not one of them asked a question of the guy."

Clearly, Kanye had initiated an important dialogue in America. And apparently, he didn't regret what he had said, because two days later, on Ellen DeGeneres's show, he underlined his original statements with these remarks:

"They have been trying to sweep us [African-Americans] under the kitchen sink and it was so in people's faces and so on TV . . . that they couldn't even hide it any more. Down there, people are living below the poverty level to start off with, before this happened. A year ago I was on tour with Usher and we had a hurricane hit Florida and everybody was saying, 'If this hurricane went to Louisiana, if it went to Mississippi, they wouldn't be able to handle it.' [That was] a year ago—and there was nothing done about it."

Still, the reaction to his ad-lib comments took Kanye by surprise. The Celebrity Blog reported that he said:

"What surprised me most was the impact of my voice on NBC. It's just magical that I can say something that's

a popular opinion and it really has an impact. I didn't think about Bush until the telethon. I saw him [on TV]— I'm like, 'Wait a second, dude, that guy over there, he doesn't care.' But America was already headed that way. I think it was a common opinion."

In Kanye's mind, his comments about President Bush took far less guts than did his statements during an MTV interview where he called for hip-hop to put an end to its **homophobia**. Kanye, who has a homosexual cousin, was ashamed of his own prejudice—and he called for rappers to stop their gay-bashing. Soon after the interview, rumors arose that Kanye was himself gay. "I knew there would be a backlash," Kanye told *Rolling Stone*, "but it didn't scare me, because I felt like God wanted me to say something about that."

Outrageous Kanye

Many people are annoyed by Kanye's brash personality and outspoken comments. Others just plain don't like him and openly criticize both his ego and his music. When he appeared on the cover of *Rolling Stone* with a crown of thorns on his head, looking like an African American version of Jesus Christ from Mel Gibson's *The Passion*, there were plenty of people who shook their heads in exasperation. They accused Kanye of having a Messiah complex. After all, when you start confusing yourself with the Savior of the world, you're taking a pretty outrageous stand! Critics pointed out that Kanye's life hasn't really been all that difficult: the child of middle-class professionals, he's never known true poverty, and he's certainly never had to experience much failure. What difficulties he has had to face, these critics point out, have been Kanye's own doing (like the controversy over his statements after Hurricane Katrina).

And yes, it's true: Kanye West is outrageous. But part of the outrage he inspires is caused by the fact that he's never afraid to shout the truth. Whether he's condemning South African diamond mines for their abuse of black miners or speaking out against rap music's poor treatment of women, Kanye always stands up for what is right. When he sees anything he perceives as hypocrisy or injustice, he points his finger—and whenever he recognizes that he's a part of the problem, he's not afraid to turn that same condemning finger on himself.

CAT POWER + JAMES BLUNT + BILLY JOEL

RollingStone

rollingstone.com
Issue 993 >> February 9, 2006 >> $3.95

BODE MILLER
Out of Control

GOD'S SENATOR
Inside the War Room of the Religious Right

BATTLESTAR GALACTICA
The Toughest, Smartest Show On Television

WILSON PICKETT
1941-2006

THE PASSION of KANYE WEST

To some, it seems as though Kanye spends much of his time seeking controversy. In February 2006, a photo of Kanye posing as Jesus appeared on the *Rolling Stone* cover. Kanye says he has a lot in common with Jesus, but not everyone agrees.

Despite the controversy that often surrounds him, Kanye West is a role model to many young people all over the world. In recognition of his good works, Kanye received the Million Man March Image Award in 2005.

Kanye the Role Model

When the Honorable Minister Louis Farrakhan initiated his Million Man March (MMM) movement, he called on black men to be strong and moral leaders. The MMM movement works to encourage African Americans to get out and vote and increase their involvement in **volunteerism** to improve their communities. MMM committee member Latonja Muhammad initiated an Image Award to be given in recognition of accomplishments in the fields of politics, business, religion, and entertainment. Kanye West has stood out in all four, and Minister Farrakhan recognized that Kanye West is doing his best to be a role model for the black community. On February 27, 2005, Farrakhan awarded Kanye the Million Man March Image Award.

Does all this go to Kanye's head? Of course. But still, he says his goals for the future are simple. He told *Blender* magazine that he's "trying to become more comfortable with the position I'm in." With typical Kanye confidence, he concluded, "The last album was groundbreaking. Now the process is to strive for greatness."

The *Blender* article offered Kanye's advice for us all: "If you can express yourself . . . do it."

Kanye concludes, "I just want to keep being creative and keep coming up with things that the world is missing."

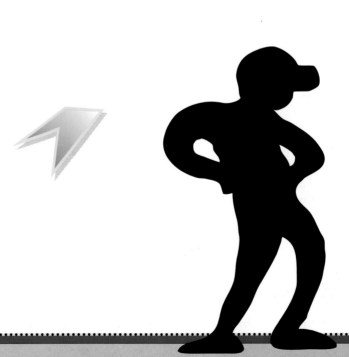

1977   Kanye West is born on June 8 in Atlanta, Georgia.

1997   Coproduces tracks for Harlem World and Mad Rapper.

2002   Tells Oprah Winfrey that he'll be on her show one day.

2002   Is involved in a near-fatal car accident.

2004   First CD, *College Dropout*, is released.

2005   Appears on *Oprah* and Barbara Walters' *Most Fascinating People of the Year*.

       Releases *Late Registration*.

       Kanye West Foundation program Loop Dream is introduced into five schools.

       Wins five Grammy Awards.

       Chicago mayor declares February 27 Kanye West Day.

       Receives the Million Man March Image Award.

       Performs at Live 8 concert in Philadelphia.

       Appears on the cover of *Time* magazine.

       Goes "off-script" to criticize President Bush during an NBC telethon for hurricane relief; he repeats his comments a few days later on Ellen DeGeneres's show.

2006   Appears as Jesus Christ on the cover of *Rolling Stone*.

       Wins three Grammy Awards.

Discography

Solo Albums

2004   *College Dropout*

2005   *Late Registration*

Number-One Singles:

2004   "Slow Jamz"

2005   "Gold Digger"

Television Appearances

2002   *Driven*

2003   *9th Annual Soul Train Lady of Soul Awards*; *Russell Simmons Presents Def Poetry*

2004   *Chappelle's Show*; *4th Annual BET Awards*; *Fuse 100%*; *The 2004 Billboard Music Awards*; *The 2004 World Music Awards*; *MOBO Awards*; *MTV Video Music Awards*; *Punk'd*; *Raymann is laat"*; *Russell Simmons Presents Def Poetry*; *Tavis Smiley*; *The Sharon Osbourne Show*; *Total Request Live*; *Jimmy Kimmel Live*; *Top of the Pops*; *Live with Regis and Kelly*

2005   *American Express Jam Sessions*; *Block Party*; *A Concert for Hurricane Relief*; *Driven*; *The 47th Annual Grammy Awards*; *Kathy Griffin: My Life on the D-List*; *Saturday Night Live*; *2nd Annual VH1 Hip-Hop Honors*; *Friday Night with Jonathan Ross*; *MTV Music Awards 2005*; *Russell Simmons Presents Def Poetry*; *36th NAACP Image Awards*; *VH1 Big in 05*; *The Charlie Rose Show*; *Cribs*; *106 & Park Top 10 Live*; *Top of the Pops*; *CD: UK*; *Oprah*

2006   *Ellen: The Ellen DeGeneres Show*; *The 48th Annual Grammy Awards*

Film

2004   *Fade to Black*

2005   *State Property 2*

Video

2003   *Through the Wire*

2004   *All Falls Down*

        Jesus Walks

        Jesus Walks (version 2)

        Jesus Walks (version 3)

        The New Workout Plan

2005   *The Art of 16 Bars: Get Ya' Bars Up*

        Be

        Diamonds from Sierra Leone

        Gold Digger

        John Legend: Get Lifted

        John Legend: Live at the House of Blues

        Kanye West: College Dropout—Video Anthology

        The MC: Why We Do It

Awards

2004   Wins Billboard Music Awards for Rap Artist of the Year, Rap Artist of the Year, and New R&B/Hip-Hop Artist of the Year

        Wins Mobo Awards for Best Album, Best Producer, and Best Hip Hop Act

        Wins Source Awards for Album of the Year, Video of the Year, and Breakthrough Artist

2005   Wins BET Awards for Best Male Hip-Hop and Video of the Year

        Wins Billboard Artist Achievement Award

        Wins BMI Urban Award for Producer of the Year

        Wins MTV Video Music Award for Best Male Video

        Wins NAACP Image Award for Outstanding New Artist

Wins TRL Award for Best New Artist

Wins Vibe Award for Best Rapper

Wins XM Nation Music Award for Urban Artist of the Year

Wins Grammy Awards for Best Rap Album, Best Rap Song, and Best R&B Song (as producer)

Receives the Million Man March Image Award

2006   Wins Meteor Ireland Music Award for Best International Male

Wins Grammy Awards for Best Rap Album, Best Rap Song, and Best Rap Solo Performance

Books

Chang, Jeff. *Can't Stop, Won't Stop: A History of the Hip-Hop Generation.* New York: St. Martin's Press, 2005.

Kulkarni, Neil. *Hip Hop: Bring the Noise (Stories Behind Every Song).* New York: Thunder's Mouth Press, 2004.

Nelson, George. *Hip-Hop America.* New York: Penguin, 2005.

Rose, Tricia. *Black Noise: Rap Music and Black Culture in Contemporary America.* Middletown, Conn.: Wesleyan University Press, 2004.

Magazines

Davis, Kimberly. "Kanye West: Hip-Hop's New Big Shot." *Ebony*, April 2005.

Norris, Chris. "Top of the World." *Blender*, September 2005.

Ogunnaike, Lola. "West World." *Rolling Stone*, February 9, 2006.

Valby, Karen. "The Ego Has Landed." *Entertainment Weekly*, February 3, 2006.

Web Sites

Hip-Hop Summit Action Network Manager
www.hsan.org

Kanye West Fan Site
www.kanyewest.org

The Kanye West Foundation
www.kanyewestfoundation.com

Official Kanye West Site
www.kanyewest.com

activist—someone who vigorously and sometimes aggressively pursues a political or social goal.

Black Panthers—a late 1960s, early 1970s militant African American political group opposed to white domination.

cliché—a phrase or word that has lost its original effectiveness from overuse.

conservatives—those reluctant to change, preferring the status quo.

delving—investigating or researching something thoroughly.

gangsta rap—a style of rap music that portrays an outlaw lifestyle of sex, drugs, and violence.

homophobia—an irrational hatred or fear of homosexuality, gay and lesbian people, and their culture.

initiative—a plan or strategy designed to deal with a particular problem.

materialistic—concerned with material wealth and possessions.

mentor—someone who provides advice and support to someone less experienced.

perfectionist—someone who demands perfection in all things, especially his or her own work.

protégé—a young or less experienced person who receives advice and guidance from someone more experienced.

R&B—rhythm and blues; a mixing of blues and jazz.

racism—prejudice against people who belong to other races.

ramifications—unintended results of an action.

rap—a style of popular music characterized by spoken vocals and often featuring a looped electronic beat in the background.

samplers—electronic devices that allow sound to be manipulated on a computer.

stereotypes—generalizations about someone based on incomplete, often inaccurate information.

subculture—a separate social group within a larger culture and that usually has ideas and practices that differ from those of the larger group.

vintage—representing what is best or most typical of something.

volunteerism—the practice of using volunteers in community service organizations and programs.

Rae Simons is a flexible author who has written everything from romance novels to children's books. She says what she likes best about writing educational books is the opportunity to learn about new ideas she might not otherwise have considered. She has written for Mason Crest on a variety of topics, including careers with character and the European Union.

Picture Credits

page

 2: KRT/Lionel Hahn
 8: KRT/Hahn Khayat
11: KRT/Lionel Hahn
12: Jean Catuffe / Sipa
13: Timothy A. Clary/AFP/ Getty Images
14: Tsuni/Gamma
16: Laura Farr/AdMedia
18: NMI Archives
21: KRT/Richard Corkery
22: Zuma Press/Sven Darmer
24: FPS/NMI
27: Zuma Press/Nancy Kaszerman
28: Zuma Press/Lora Voigt

30: KRT/Lionel Hahn
33: AP Photo/Kevork Djansezian
35: NMI/Michelle Feng
36: PRNewsFoto/NMI
39: Zuma Press/Rob DeLorenzo
40: Darla Khazei/WENN
42: Zuma Press
45: PNP/WENN
46: Hill Sabre/SIPA
47: Reuters/Jim Ruymen
49: Reuters/Fred Prouser
50: Jr Davis/Photoline
53: WENN
54: PRNewsFoto/NMI

Front cover: KRT/Hahn Khayat
Back cover: Roca John/Gamma